To:

· ·

From:

· ·

Date:

· ·

101 Words that Matter Most for Mothers

© 2012 Christian Art Gifts, RSA
        Christian Art Gifts Inc., IL, USA

Designed by Christian Art Gifts

Images used under license from Shutterstock.com

Scripture quotations marked NIV are taken from the *Holy Bible*, New International Version® NIV®. Copyright © 1973, 1978, 1984, 2011 by International Bible Society. Used by permission of Zondervan Publishing House. All rights reserved.

Scripture quotations marked NLT are taken from the *Holy Bible*, New Living Translation®, second edition. Copyright © 1996, 2004, 2007 by Tyndale House Publishers, Inc., Carol Stream, Illinois 60188. All rights reserved.

Scripture quotations marked MSG are taken from THE MESSAGE. Copyright © by Eugene H. Peterson, 1993, 1994, 1995, 1996, 2000, 2001, 2002 by NavPress Publishing Group. Used by permission.

Scripture quotations marked ESV are taken from the *Holy Bible*, English Standard Version. Copyright © 2001 by Crossway Bibles, a division of Good News Publishers. Used by permission. All rights reserved.

Scripture quotations marked NCV are taken from the *Holy Bible*, New Century Version®. Copyright © 1987, 1988, 1991, 2005 by Word Publishing, a division of Thomas Nelson, Inc. Used by permission.

Printed in China

ISBN 978-1-4321-0163-3

15 16 17 18 19 20 21 22 23 24 – 12 11 10 9 8 7 6 5 4 3

101
Words that Matter Most
for *Mothers*

christian
art gifts®

Contents

.........❧.........

Abundance

a · bun · dance /əˈbʌndəns/ *noun*

1. A very large quantity of something. 2. The state or condition of having a copious quantity of something; plentifulness. 3. Prosperity. 4. A great or plentiful amount. 5. Fullness to over-flowing.

Grace and peace be yours in abundance.
- *2 Pet. 1:2 NIV* -

The Lord will open to you His good treasury, the heavens, to give the rain to your land in its season and to bless all the work of your hands.
- *Deut. 28:12 ESV* -

"I have come that they may have life, and have it to the full."
- *John 10:10 NIV* -

The abundant life does not come to those who have had a lot of obstacles removed from their path by others. It develops from within and is rooted in strong mental and moral fiber.
- *William Mather Lewis* -

Accountability

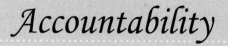

ac · count · a · bi · li · ty /əˌkaʊntəˈbɪləti/ *noun*

1. The fact or condition of being accountable; responsibility. 2. Liable to being called to account; answerable.

"And I tell you this, you must give an account on judgment day for every idle word you speak."
- Matt. 12:36 NLT -

It's wonderful to be young! Enjoy every minute of it. Do everything you want to do; take it all in. But remember that you must give an account to God for everything you do.
- Eccles. 11:9 NLT -

The godly are directed by honesty.
- Prov. 11:5 NLT -

Accountability breeds response-ability.
- Stephen R. Covey -

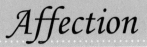

Affection

af · fec · tion/əˈfekʃn/*noun*

1. A tender feeling toward another; fondness.
2. Feeling or emotion. 3. A disposition to feel, do, or say; a propensity.

Love one another with brotherly affection.
Outdo one another in showing honor.
- *Rom. 12:10* ESV -

His divine power has given us everything we need
for life and godliness through our knowledge of
Him who called us by His own glory and goodness.
- *2 Pet. 1:3* NIV -

The Lord is righteous in all
His ways and kind in all His works.
- *Ps. 145:17* ESV -

Affection is responsible for nine-tenths of whatever
solid and durable happiness there is in our lives.
- *C. S Lewis* -

Ambition

am · bi · tion/æmˈbɪʃn/*noun*

1. An eager or strong desire to achieve something. 2. Desire for exertion or activity; energy, strong desire for success, achievement, or distinction. 3. Goal; aim, aspiration, dream, ambitiousness, drive, aspirations, power.

In all your ways acknowledge the Lord,
and He will make your paths straight.
- Prov. 3:6 NIV *-*

May God grant your heart's desires
and make all your plans succeed.
- Ps. 20:4 NLT *-*

It is God who works in you to will
and to act according to His good purpose.
- Phil. 2:13 NIV *-*

All who have accomplished great things have had a great aim, have fixed their gaze on a goal which was high, one which sometimes seemed impossible.
- Orison Swett Marden -

Appearance

ap · pear · ance /əˈpɪərəns/ *noun*

1. The outward or visible aspect of a person or thing. 2. Look, face, form, air, figure, image, looks, bearing, aspect, manner, expression.

You know me inside and out, You know every bone in my body; You know exactly how I was made, bit by bit, how I was sculpted from nothing into something.
- Ps. 139:15 MSG -

"Do not be afraid, for I have ransomed you. I have called you by name; you are Mine."
- Isa. 43:1 NLT -

You are judging by appearances. If anyone is confident that they belong to Christ, they should consider again that we belong to Christ just as much as they do.
- 2 Cor. 10:7 NIV -

Don't rely too much on labels.
Far too often they are fables.

- Charles H. Spurgeon -

Appreciation

ap·pre·ci·a·tion /ə,priːʃiˈeɪʃn/ *noun*

**1. Recognition of the quality, value, significance, or magnitude of people and things.
2. A judgment or opinion, especially a favorable one. 3. An expression of gratitude.**

Give thanks in all circumstances; for this is
the will of God in Christ Jesus for you.
- *1 Thess. 5:18* ESV -

Since everything God created is good,
we should not reject any of it. We may
receive it gladly, with thankful hearts.
- *1 Tim. 4:4* NLT -

No matter what happens, always
be thankful, for this is God's will
for you who belong to Jesus Christ.
- *1 Thess. 5:18* NLT -

Feeling appreciated is one of the most important
needs that people have. When you share with someone your appreciation and gratitude, they will not forget you. Appreciation will return to you many times.
- *Steve Brunkhorst* -

Beauty

beau · ty /ˈbjuːti / *noun*

1. The quality that gives pleasure to the mind or senses and is associated with such properties as excellence of artistry, truthfulness, and originality. 2. One that is beautiful, especially a beautiful woman. 3. An outstanding or conspicuous example, brilliant radiant beauty, exquisiteness.

.... ❀ ....

Your beauty should not come from outward adornment. Rather, it should be that of your inner self, the unfading beauty of a gentle and quiet spirit, which is of great worth in God's sight.
- *1 Pet. 3:3-4 NIV -*

Charm is deceptive, and beauty is fleeting; but a woman who fears the Lord is to be praised.
- *Prov. 31:30 NIV -*

The Lord doesn't see things the way you see them. People judge by outward appearance, but the Lord looks at the heart.
- *1 Sam. 16:7 NLT -*

Taking joy in living is a woman's best cosmetic.
- Rosalind Russell -

Bible

bi · ble/ˈbaɪbl/*noun*

1. God's message to believers including the books of the Old Testament and the New Testament. 2. Guide, Compass, Good Book, Holy Scripture, Scripture, Word of God, Word.

·········  ·········

God's Word is true,
and everything He does is right.
- Ps. 33:4 NCV -

The Word of God is living and active. Sharper than
any double-edged sword, it penetrates even
to dividing soul and spirit, joints and marrow;
it judges the thoughts and attitudes of the heart.
- Heb. 4:12 NIV -

Your word is like a lamp for
my feet and a light for my path.
- Ps. 119:105 NCV -

The Bible is the inevitable outcome of God's
continuous speech. It is the infallible declaration
of His mind ... put into our familiar human words.
- A. W. Tozer -

Blessings

bless · ings/'blesɪŋs/*noun*

1. The act of invoking divine protection or aid
2. The words or ceremony used for this 3. Approval, good wishes, the bestowal of a divine gift or favor.

Blessed are those who trust in the Lord and have made the Lord their hope and confidence.
- *Jer. 17:7 NLT* -

May the Lord bless you and protect you. May the Lord smile on you and be gracious to you. May the Lord show you His favor and give you His peace.
- *Num. 6:24-26 NLT* -

God has showered you with blessings.
- *Ps. 116:7 MSG* -

For today and its blessings,
I owe the world an attitude of gratitude.

- *Anonymous* -

Boldness

bold · ness/ˈboʊldnəs/*adjective*

1. Fearless and daring; courageous. 2. Requiring or exhibiting courage and bravery. 3. The trait of being willing to undertake things that involve risk or danger, adventurousness.

....  ....

We can say with confidence,
"The Lord is my helper, so I will have no fear.
What can mere people do to me?"
- Heb. 13:6 NLT -

"Fear not, for I am with you; be not
dismayed, for I am your God; I will
strengthen you, I will help you, I will
uphold you with My righteous right hand."
- Isa. 41:10 ESV -

Overwhelming victory is ours
through Christ, who loved us.
- Rom. 8:37 NLT -

Freedom lies in being bold.
- Robert Frost -

Challenges

chal · lenges/'tʃælɪndʒs/*noun*

**1. A test of one's abilities or resources in a
demanding but stimulating undertaking.
2. To make demands on; stimulate.**

"Call to Me and I will answer you and tell you
great and unsearchable things you do not know."
- Jer. 33:3 NIV -

"I am the Lord, your God, who takes
hold of your right hand and says to you,
'Do not fear; I will help you.'"
- Isa. 41:13 NIV -

When I was a child, I spoke and thought
and reasoned as a child. But when I
grew up, I put away childish things.
- 1 Cor. 13:11 NLT -

Opportunities to find deeper powers within
ourselves come when life seems most challenging.
- Joseph Campbell -

Character

char · ac · ter /kærəktər/ *noun*

1. The combination of qualities or features that distinguishes one person from another. 2. Moral or ethical strength. 3. A description of a person's attributes, traits, or abilities. 4. Reputation, personality, nature, temperament, individuality.

....  ....

Make it your goal to live a quiet life, minding your own business and working with your hands, just as we instructed you before. Then people who are not Christians will respect the way you live, and you will not need to depend on others.
- 1 Thess. 4:11-12 NLT -

When the Holy Spirit controls our lives, He will produce this kind of fruit in us: love, joy, peace, patience, kindness, goodness, faithfulness, gentleness, and self-control.
- Gal. 5:22-23 NLT -

God is working in you, giving you the desire to obey Him and the power to do what pleases Him.
- Phil. 2:13 NLT -

Your life may be the only Bible some people read.
- Anonymous -

Children

chil · dren /ˈtʃɪldrən/ *noun*

1. **A son or daughter, brood, offspring, family.**
2. **A member of a tribe; descendant, kids, minors.**
3. **A mother loves her children unconditionally.**

....  ....

Children are a gift from the Lord;
babies are a reward.
- *Ps. 127:3 NCV* -

"Whoever embraces one of these children
as I do embraces Me, and far more
than Me – God who sent Me."
- *Mark 9:36-37 MSG* -

"I prayed for this child, and the Lord
has granted me what I asked of Him.
So now I give him to the Lord. For his
whole life he will be given over to the Lord."
- *1 Sam. 1:27-28 NIV* -

The soul is healed by being with children.
- *Fyodor Dostoevsky* -

Choices

choi · ces /tʃɔɪses/ *noun*

1. The act of choosing. 2. The power, right, or liberty to choose. 3. A number or variety from which to choose. 4. An alternative, option, preference, selection.

··········  ··········

"Choose to love the Lord your God and to obey Him and to commit yourself to Him, for He is your life."
- *Deut. 30:20* NLT -

"Anyone who chooses to do the will of God will find out whether My teaching comes from God or whether I speak on My own."
- *John 7:17* NIV -

"You did not choose Me, but I chose you and appointed you so that you might go and bear fruit – fruit that will last – and so that whatever you ask in My name the Father will give you."
- *John 15:16* NIV -

The hardest thing to learn in life is which bridge to cross and which to burn.
- *David Russell* -

Comfort

com · fort/ˈkʌmfərt/*tr. verb*

**1. To soothe in time of affliction or distress.
2. To ease physically; relieve, console,
encourage, cheer, strengthen, reassure,
hearten. 3. Solace in time of grief or fear.**

········· ❀ ·········

May our Lord Jesus Christ Himself and
God our Father, who loved us and by
His grace gave us eternal comfort and a
wonderful hope, comfort you and strengthen
you in every good thing you do and say.
- *2 Thess. 2:16-17* NLT -

God is our merciful Father and the source
of all comfort. He comforts us in all our
troubles so that we can comfort others.
When they are troubled, we will be able to
give them the same comfort God has given us.
- *2 Cor. 1:3-4* NLT -

God heals the brokenhearted
and binds up their wounds.
- *Ps. 147:3* NIV -

The sun can break through the darkest cloud;
love can brighten the gloomiest day.

- *William Arthur Ward* -

Compassion

com · pas · sion /kəmˈpæʃn/ *noun*

1. Deep awareness of the suffering of another coupled with the wish to relieve it. 2. Sharing the feelings of others (especially feelings of sorrow or anguish) 3. Deep awareness of and sympathy for another's suffering. 4. Mercy, tenderness, pity.

The Lord your God is gracious
and compassionate. He will not turn
His face from you if you return to Him.
- 2 Chron. 30:9 NIV -

Because of the Lord's great love we are not
consumed, for His compassions never fail. They
are new every morning; great is Your faithfulness.
- Lam. 3:22-23 NIV -

The Lord is good to everyone.
He showers compassion on all His creation.
- Ps. 145:9 NLT -

The best exercise for strengthening the
heart is reaching down and lifting people up.
- Ernest Blevins -

Confidence

con · fi · dence /ˈkɑːnfɪdəns/ *noun*

**1. A feeling of trust in a person or thing.
2. Belief in one's own abilities; self-assurance.
3. Freedom from doubt. 4. A state of confident
hopefulness that events will be favorable.
5. Trust, belief, faith, dependence.**

Being confident of this, that He who began
a good work in you will carry it on to
completion until the day of Christ Jesus.
- *Phil. 1:6 NIV* -

It is better to trust the Lord
than to put confidence in princes.
- *Ps. 118:8 NLT* -

The Lord will be your confidence
and will keep your foot from being snared.
- *Prov. 3:26 ESV* -

God expects of us this one thing that glorifies Him –
and that is to remain absolutely confident in Him,
remembering what He has said beforehand,
and being sure that His purposes will be fulfilled.

- *Oswald Chambers* -

Contentment

con · tent · ment/kən'tentmənt/*noun*

1. The state of being contented; satisfaction.
2. Peace, ease, pleasure, comfort, happiness,
fulfillment, gratification, serenity, contented-
ness. 3. Happiness with one's situation in life.

....  ....

I have learned in whatever situation
I am to be content. I can do all things
through Him who strengthens me.
- Phil. 4:11, 13 ESV -

If they obey and serve Him, they will
spend the rest of their days in prosperity
and their years in contentment.
- Job 36:11 NIV -

So be content with who you are, and don't
put on airs. God's strong hand is on you;
He'll promote you at the right time. Live carefree
before God; He is most careful with you.
- 1 Pet. 5:6 MSG -

True contentment is a thing as active as agriculture.
It is the power of getting out of any situation all
that there is in it. It is arduous and it is rare.
- G. K. Chesterton -

Courage

cour · age/ˈkɜːrɪdʒ/*noun*

1. The power or quality of dealing with or facing danger, fear or pain. 2. A quality of spirit that enables you to face danger or pain without showing fear. 3. Braveness, bravery.

"Be strong and courageous!
Do not be afraid or discouraged.
For the Lord your God is with
you wherever you go."
- *Josh. 1:9* NLT -

Having hope will give you courage.
You will be protected and will rest in safety.
- *Job 11:18* NLT -

In Your strength I can crush an army;
with my God I can scale any wall.
- *Ps. 18:29* NLT -

Our faith does not lie in trusting
God to stop the storm but in trusting
Him to enable us to walk through the storm.

- *Jill Briscoe* -

Decisiveness

de · ci · sive · ness /dɪˈsaɪsɪvnəs/ *adjective*

1. Conclusive, crucial, definitive, determinative. 2. Determining or having the power to determine an outcome. 3. Firmness of purpose, resoluteness.

....  ....

God guides us with our big decisions.
- *Ps. 23:3* NLT -

The Lord will guide you always.
- *Isa. 58:11* NIV -

"I will lead the blind by ways they have not known,
along unfamiliar paths I will guide them;
I will turn the darkness into light before
them and make the rough places smooth."
- *Isa. 42:16* NIV -

Every time you make a choice you are turning the
central part of you, the part that chooses, into
something a little different than what it was before.
- *C. S. Lewis* -

Discernment

dis · cern · ment /dɪˈsɜːrnmənt/ *noun*

1. The act or process of exhibiting keen insight and good judgment. 2. Savvy, understanding, apprehension. 4. The trait of judging wisely and objectively, discretion, wisdom.

"I will give you a wise and discerning heart,
so that there will never have been anyone like you."
- *1 Kings 3:12* NIV -

The heart of the discerning acquires
knowledge; the ears of the wise seek it out.
- *Prov. 18:15* NIV -

Happy is the person who … gains understanding.
- *Prov. 3:13* NLT -

Discernment is not a matter of simply telling the difference between right and wrong; rather it is telling the difference between right and almost right.

- *Charles H. Spurgeon* -

Discipline

dis · ci · pline/ˈdɪsəplɪn/*noun*

**1. Training expected to produce a specific character or pattern of behavior, especially training that produces moral or mental improvement.
2. Controlled behavior resulting from disciplinary training; self-control. 3. A systematic method to obtain obedience. 4. Punishment intended to correct or train.**

.... ❀ ....

Discipline your children; you'll be glad you did – they'll turn out delightful to live with.
- Prov. 29:17 MSG -

No discipline is enjoyable while it is happening – it is painful! But afterward there will be a quiet harvest of right living for those who are trained in this way.
- Heb. 12:11 NLT -

You should realize that just as a parent disciplines a child, the Lord your God disciplines you to help you. So obey the commands of the Lord your God by walking in His ways and fearing Him.
- Deut. 8:5-6 NLT -

Discipline is the refining fire by which talent becomes ability.
- Roy L. Smith -

Encouragement

en · cour · age · ment /ɪnˈkɜːrɪdʒmənt/ *noun*

1. The act of encouraging. 2. The state of being encouraged. 3. One that encourages. 4. Inspiration, help, support, aid, comfort.

·········  ·········

"Be strong and courageous. Do not be afraid or terrified because of them, for the Lord your God goes with you; He will never leave you nor forsake you."
- *Deut. 31:6* NIV -

God our Father loved us and by His grace gave us eternal encouragement and good hope.
- *2 Thess. 2:16* NIV -

May our Lord Jesus Christ Himself and God our Father encourage you and strengthen you in every good thing you do and say. God loved us, and through His grace He gave us a good hope and encouragement that continues forever.
- *2 Thess. 2:16-17* NCV -

Encouragement costs you nothing to give,
but it is priceless to receive.
- *Anonymous* -

Endurance

en · du · rance/ɪnˈdʊrəns/*noun*

1. The act, quality, or power of withstanding hardship or stress. 2. The state or fact of persevering. 3. Strength, stamina, staying power, toughness, determination.

God blesses those who patiently endure testing and temptation. Afterward they will receive the crown of life that God has promised to those who love Him.
- James 1:12 NLT -

You need to persevere so that when you have done the will of God, you will receive what He has promised.
- Heb. 10:36 NIV -

"The one who endures to the end will be saved."
- Matt. 24:13 ESV -

When odds are one in a million, be that one.
- Anonymous -

Example

ex·am·ple/ɪgˈzæmpl/*noun*

1. One that is representative of a group as a whole, God's model for others to copy, role model. 2. One serving as a pattern of a specific kind. 3. A person, action, or thing that is worthy of imitation; pattern, good example, exemplar.

....  ....

Set an example for the believers in speech, in life, in love, in faith and in purity. Watch your life and doctrine closely. Persevere in them, because if you do, you will save both yourself and your hearers.
- 1 Tim. 4:12, 16 NIV -

In everything set them an example by doing what is good. In your teaching show integrity, seriousness and soundness of speech that cannot be condemned.
- Titus 2:7-8 NIV -

Follow my example, as I follow
the example of Christ.
- 1 Cor. 11:1 NIV -

Let us preach You, dear Jesus, without preaching. Not by words, but by our example. By the casting force, the sympathetic influence of what we do, the evident fullness of the love our hearts bear to You.

- Mother Teresa -

Excellence

ex·cel·lence/'eksələns/*noun*

1. The state, quality, or condition of excelling; superiority. 2. Something in which one excels, extreme merit. 3. An action, characteristic or feature in which a person excels. 4. High quality, worth, distinction, virtue, goodness, perfection, purity, greatness.

....  ....

Whatever is true, whatever is noble, whatever is right, whatever is pure, whatever is lovely, whatever is admirable – if anything is excellent or praiseworthy – think about such things.
- *Phil. 4:8* NIV -

You can make this choice by loving the Lord your God, obeying Him, and committing yourself firmly to Him. This is the key to your life.
- *Deut. 30:20* NLT -

Whatever you do, do it all for the glory of God.
- *1 Cor. 10:31* NIV -

The quality of a person's life is in direct proportion to their commitment to excellence, regardless of their chosen field of endeavor.
- *Vince Lombardi* -

Faithfulness

faith·ful·ness /ˈfeɪθflnəs/ *noun*

1. The quality of being faithful. 2. Adhering firmly and devotedly to someone or something that elicits or demands one's fidelity. 3. Trustworthiness, devotion, dependability, loyalty, trueness, steadfastness.

We live by faith, not by sight.
- *2 Cor. 5:7 NIV -*

Let us draw near to God with a sincere heart in full assurance of faith. Let us hold unswervingly to the hope we profess, for He who promised is faithful.
- *Heb. 10:22-23 NIV -*

Faith is being sure of what we hope for
and certain of what we do not see.
- *Heb. 11:1 NIV -*

A little faith will bring your soul to heaven,
but a lot of faith will bring heaven to your soul.
- *Charles H. Spurgeon -*

Family

fam · i · ly /ˈfæməli/ *noun*

1. A fundamental social group in society typically consisting of one or two parents and their children. 2. Two or more people who share goals and values, have long-term commitments to one another, and usually reside in the same dwelling place. 3. All the members of a household under one roof.

How great is the love the Father has lavished on us, that we should be called children of God! And that is what we are!
- 1 John 3:1 NIV -

"I will be a Father to you, and you will be My sons and daughters," says the Lord Almighty.
- 2 Cor. 6:18 NIV -

I bow in prayer before the Father from whom every family in heaven and on earth gets its true name.
- Eph. 3:14-15 NCV -

Other things may change us,
but we start and end with family.
- Anthony Brandt -

Finances

fi · nanc · es /ˈfaɪnænses/ *noun*
1. The management of money, banking, investments, and credit. 2. Monetary resources; funds. 3. Assets in the form of money, cash in hand, funds, monetary resource.

.... ❀ ....

"I tell you, do not be anxious about your life, what you will eat or what you will drink, nor about your body, what you will put on. Is not life more than food, and the body more than clothing?"
- *Matt. 6:25 ESV* -

"Bring your full tithe to the Temple treasury so there will be ample provisions in My Temple. Test Me in this and see if I don't open up heaven itself to you and pour out blessings beyond your wildest dreams."
- *Mal. 3:10 MSG* -

Honor God with everything you own;
give Him the first and the best. Your barns
will burst, your wine vats will brim over.
- *Prov. 3:9-10 MSG* -

The real measure of your wealth is how much
you'd be worth if you lost all your money.

- *Anonymous* -

Forgiveness

for · give · ness /fərˈgɪvnəs/ *noun*

1. The act of forgiving or the state of being forgiven 2. Willingness to forgive. 3. Compassionate feelings that support a willingness to forgive, mercifulness, mercy. The act of excusing a mistake or offense.

·········  ·········

If we confess our sins, He will forgive our sins, because we can trust God to do what is right. He will cleanse us from all the wrongs we have done.
- 1 John 1:9 NCV -

"I will forgive their wrongdoings, and I will never again remember their sins," says the Lord.
- Heb. 8:12 NLT -

"Come now, let us reason together," says the Lord. "Though your sins are like scarlet, they shall be as white as snow; though they are red as crimson, they shall be like wool."
- Isa. 1:18 NIV -

Two works of mercy set a person free: forgive and you will be forgiven, and give and you will receive.
- St. Augustine -

Friendship

friend · ship/frendʃɪp/*noun*

**1. The quality or condition of being friends.
2. A friendly relationship. 3. Friendliness;
good will. 4. Companionship, fellowship,
society, company.**

A real friend sticks closer than a brother.
- *Prov. 18:24 NLT* -

Laugh with your happy friends when they're
happy; share tears when they're down.
Get along with each other. Make friends
with nobodies; don't be the great somebody.
- *Rom. 12:16 MSG* -

Two are better than one ... if one falls down,
his friend can help him up.
- *Eccles. 4:9-10 NIV* -

A faithful friend is an image of God.

- *French Proverb* -

Fruitfulness

fruit · ful · ness /ˈfruːtfəlnəs/ *noun*

1. Produce the quality of something that causes or assists healthy growth, fertility, richness, productiveness, productivity. 2. The quality of being productive.

·········  ·········

"I am the vine; you are the branches. Those who remain in Me, and I in them, will produce much fruit."
- *John 15:5* NLT -

May you always be filled with the fruit of your salvation – the righteous character produced in your life by Christ Jesus – for this will bring much glory and praise to God.
- *Phil. 1:11* NLT -

Let us not grow weary of doing good, for in due season we will reap, if we do not give up.
- *Gal. 6:9* ESV -

The amount of time we spend with Jesus – meditating on His Word and His majesty, seeking His face – establishes our fruitfulness in the kingdom.
- *Charles Stanley* -

Fulfillment

ful · fill · ment/fʊlˈfɪlmənt/*noun*

**1. A feeling of satisfaction at having achieved
your desires. 2. Consummation, self-fulfillment,
self-realization.**

The Lord will fulfill His purpose for me;
Your steadfast love, O Lord, endures forever.
Do not forsake the work of Your hands.
- *Ps. 138:8* ESV -

"I came to give life – life in all its fullness."
- *John 10:10* NCV -

I have learned in whatever situation
I am to be content. I can do all things
through Him who strengthens me.
- *Phil. 4:11, 13* ESV -

Look at a day when you are supremely
satisfied at the end. It's not a day when
you lounge around doing nothing; it's when
you've had everything to do, and you've done it.
- *Margaret Thatcher* -

Future

fu·ture/ˈfjuːtʃər/*noun*

1. The indefinite time yet to come. 2. Something that will happen in time to come. 3. A prospective or expected condition, especially one considered with regard to growth, advancement, or development. 4. Undetermined events that will occur in that time.

....  ....

> The Lord is all I need. He takes care of me. My share in life has been pleasant; my part has been beautiful.
> - *Ps. 16:5-6* NCV -

> Always respect the Lord. Then you will have hope for the future, and your wishes will come true.
> - *Prov. 23:17-18* NCV -

> "I know the plans I have for you," declares the Lord, "plans to prosper you and not to harm you, plans to give you hope and a future."
> - *Jer. 29:11* NIV -

God has wisely kept us in the dark concerning future events and reserved for Himself the knowledge of them, that He may train us up in a dependence upon Himself and a continued readiness for every event.

- *Matthew Henry* -

Generosity

gen·er·os·i·ty /ˌdʒenəˈrɑːsəti/ *noun*

1. Liberality in giving or willingness to give.
2. Nobility of thought or behavior. 3. Amplitude; abundance. 4. A generous act. 5. The trait of being willing to give your money or time, charitableness, bounteousness, bounty, bigheartedness.

········ ❀ ········

"Give, and you will receive. Your gift will return to you in full – pressed down, shaken together to make room for more, running over, and poured into your lap."
- *Luke 6:38* NLT -

Whoever gives to the poor will lack nothing.
- *Prov. 28:27* NLT -

"Here's the lesson: Use your worldly resources to benefit others and make friends. Then, when your earthly possessions are gone, they will welcome you to an eternal home."
- *Luke 16:9* NLT -

When we come to the end of life,
the question will be, "How much have you given?"
not "How much have you gotten?"

- *George Sweeting* -

Gentleness

gen · tle · ness /ˈdʒentlnəs/ *noun*

1. The quality of being gentle. 2. Tenderness, compassion, kindness, consideration, sympathy, sweetness, softness, mildness, kindliness.

Let your gentleness be evident to all.
The Lord is near.
- Phil. 4:5 NIV -

The fruit of the Spirit is love, joy,
peace, patience, kindness, goodness,
faithfulness, gentleness, self-control.
- Gal. 5:22-23 ESV -

Pursue righteousness and a godly life, along
with faith, love, perseverance, and gentleness.
Fight the good fight for the true faith.
- 1 Tim. 6:11-12 NLT -

Nothing is so strong as gentleness,
nothing is so gentle as real strength.
- Francis de Sales -

God

God/gaːd/*noun*

1. The perfect, omnipotent, omniscient originator and ruler of the universe. 2. The creator and ruler of the world. 3. Our heavenly Father, Abba, Great I AM, Lord.

"Be still, and know that I am God."
- *Ps. 46:10* NIV -

God is love.
- *1 John 4:16* NIV -

"I am the Alpha and the Omega, the First and the Last, the Beginning and the End."
- *Rev. 22:13* NIV -

God is not what you imagine or what you think you understand. If you understand you have failed.

- *St. Augustine* -

Goodness

good · ness/'gʊdnəs/*noun*

1. The state or quality of being good. 2. Generosity; kindness, moral excellence; piety; virtue.
3. Integrity, morality, honesty, righteousness.
4. Goodwill, mercy, compassion, kind-heartedness.

Each one should use whatever gift he has
received to serve others, faithfully
administering God's grace in its various forms.
- 1 Pet. 4:10 NIV -

"If you give even a cup of cold water to one of the
least of My followers, you will surely be rewarded."
- Matt. 10:42 NLT -

One gives freely, yet grows all the richer.
Whoever brings blessing will be enriched,
and one who waters will himself be watered.
- Prov. 11:24-25 ESV -

Goodness and hard work are rewarded with respect.
- Luther Campbell -

Grace

grace/greɪs/*noun*

1. A state of sanctification by God; the free and unmerited favor or beneficence of God; saving grace. 2. A disposition to be generous or helpful; goodwill, mercy. 3. A favor rendered by one who need not do so.

"My gracious favor is all you need.
My power works best in your weakness."
- *2 Cor. 12:9* NLT -

God is able to make all grace abound to you,
so that in all things at all times, having all that
you need, you will abound in every good work.
- *2 Cor. 9:8* NIV -

God opposes the proud,
but gives grace to the humble.
- *James 4:6* NIV -

Grace keeps us from worrying because
worry deals with the past, while grace
deals with the present and future.

- *Joyce Meyer* -

Gratitude

grat·i·tude/ˈɡrætɪtuːd/*noun*

1. The state of being grateful; thankfulness.
2. Appreciativeness, gratefulness, warm friendly feelings of gratitude.

········· ✿ ·········

Give thanks to the Lord, for He is good;
His love endures forever. Praise be to the Lord,
the God of Israel, from everlasting to everlasting.
- *1 Chron. 16:34, 36* NIV -

I'm thanking You, God, from a full heart.
I'm whistling, laughing, and jumping for joy;
I'm singing Your song, High God.
- *Ps. 9:1-2* MSG -

Since everything God created is good,
we should not reject any of it. We may
receive it gladly, with thankful hearts.
- *1 Tim. 4:4* NLT -

At times our own light goes out and is
rekindled by a spark from another person.
Each of us has cause to think with deep gratitude
of those who have lighted the flame within us.

- *Albert Schweitzer* -

Guidance

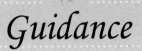

guid · ance /'gaɪdns/ *noun*

1. The act or process of guiding. 2. Something that provides direction or advice as to a decision or course of action, direction, road map, guideline.

The Lord says, "I will make you wise and show you where to go. I will guide you and watch over you."
- Ps. 32:8 NCV -

God is our God forever and ever;
He will be our guide even to the end.
- Ps. 48:14 NIV -

You will hear a voice say, "This is the way;
turn around and walk here."
- Isa. 30:21 NLT -

Seek God first in all you do – then His light
will shine on the road you should take.

- Anonymous -

Happiness

hap·pi·ness/ˈhæpɪnəs/*noun*

1. A state of well-being characterized by emotions ranging from contentment to intense joy. 2. Enjoying, showing, or marked by pleasure, satisfaction, or joy. 3. Cheerfulness, gladness, rejoicing.

....  ....

You have made known to me the path of life;
You will fill me with joy in Your presence,
with eternal pleasures at Your right hand.
- *Ps. 16:11* NIV -

Happy are the people whose God is the Lord.
- *Ps. 144:15* NCV -

A glad heart makes a happy face.
- *Prov. 15:13* NLT -

Happiness is like jam: you can't spread
it without getting some on yourself.
- *Barbara Johnson* -

Health

health/helθ/*noun*

1. The overall condition of an organism at a given time. 2. Soundness, especially of body or mind; freedom from disease or abnormality. 3. A condition of optimal well-being; strength, fitness, vigor, good condition.

Those who look to Him for help will be radiant with joy; no shadow of shame will darken their faces.
- *Ps. 34:5 NLT* -

He was wounded for our transgressions;
He was crushed for our iniquities;
upon Him was the chastisement that brought
us peace, and with His stripes we are healed.
- *Isa. 53:5 ESV* -

"I am the Lord who heals you."
- *Exod. 15:26 NCV* -

One who enjoys good health is rich in a great way.

- *Anonymous* -

Heaven

hea · ven /ˈhevn/ *noun*

1. The sky or universe as seen from the earth; the firmament. Often used in the plural. 2. The abode of God, the angels, and the souls of those who are granted salvation. 3. An eternal state of communion with God; everlasting bliss.

·········  ·········

I look up to the mountains – does my help come from there? My help comes from the Lord, who made heaven and earth!
- Ps. 121:1-2 NLT -

We have a priceless inheritance – an inheritance that is kept in heaven for you, pure and undefiled, beyond the reach of change and decay.
- 1 Pet. 1:4 NLT -

"No eye has seen, no ear has heard, and no mind has imagined what God has prepared for those who love Him."
- 1 Cor. 2:9 NLT -

Aim at heaven and you will get earth thrown in.
Aim at earth and you get neither.
- C. S. Lewis -

Home

home/houm/*noun*

1. A place where one lives; a residence. 2. An environment offering security and happiness. 3. A dwelling place together with the family or social unit that occupies it; a household. 4. Home is where the heart is, providing the ultimate comfort and security for others, a sanctuary, a nurturing environment.

········· ❀ ·········

As for me and my household,
we will serve the Lord.
- *Josh. 24:15* NIV -

Jesus replied, "All who love Me will do what I say.
My Father will love them, and We will come
and make Our home with each of them."
- *John 14:23* NLT -

Better a dry crust with peace and quiet
than a house full of feasting, with strife.
- *Prov. 17:1* NIV -

The goal of every married couple, indeed,
every Christian home, should be to make
Christ the Head, the Counselor and the Guide.

- *Paul Sadler* -

Honesty

hon · es · ty/'ɑːnəsti/*noun*

1. The quality or condition of being honest; integrity. 2. Truthfulness; sincerity. 3. Right- eousness, adhering to moral principles, moral soundness; incorruption, characterized by integrity or probity.

....  ....

You must have accurate and honest weights and measures, so that you may live long in the land the Lord your God is giving you.
- *Deut. 25:15 NIV* -

It is an honor to receive an honest reply.
- *Prov. 24:26 NLT* -

I know, my God, that You test the heart and are pleased with integrity. All these things have I given willingly and with honest intent.
- *1 Chron. 29:17 NIV* -

Be true to your work, your word, and your friend.
- *Henry David Thoreau* -

Honor

hon · or/anər/*noun*

1. High respect, as that shown for special merit; esteem. 2. Good name; reputation. 3. Glory or recognition; distinction. The quality of being honorable and having a good name. 4. Show respect towards, abide by, observe.

By His divine power, God has given us everything we need for living a godly life. We have received all of this by coming to know Him, the one who called us to Himself by means of His marvelous glory and excellence.
- *2 Pet. 1:3* NLT -

The Lord bestows favor and honor;
no good thing does He withhold
from those whose walk is blameless.
- *Ps. 84:11* NIV -

True humility and fear of the Lord
lead to riches, honor, and long life.
- *Prov. 22:4* NLT -

No person was ever honored for what he received.
Honor has been the reward for what he gave.

- *Calvin Coolidge* -

Hope

hope/hoʊp/*noun*

1. A feeling of desire for something and confidence in the possibility of its fulfillment.
2. A person or thing that gives cause for hope.
3. Belief, confidence, expectation.

Those who hope in the Lord will
renew their strength. They will soar on
wings like eagles; they will run and not
grow weary, they will walk and not be faint.
- Isa. 40:31 NIV -

Guide me in Your truth and teach me, for You are
God my Savior, and my hope is in You all day long.
- Ps. 25:5 NIV -

The Lord is good to those whose
hope is in Him, to the one who seeks Him.
Lam. 3:25 NIV -

Hope is the word which God
has written on the brow of every man.
- Victor Hugo -

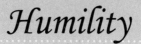

Humility

hu · mil · i · ty /hjuːˈmɪləti / *noun*

**1. The quality or condition of being humble.
2. Disposition to be humble; a lack of false
pride. 3. Meekness, modesty, submissiveness.**

Humble yourselves before the Lord,
and He will exalt you.
- *James 4:10 ESV* -

"Whoever exalts himself will be humbled,
and whoever humbles himself will be exalted."
- *Matt. 23:12 NIV* -

"Whoever humbles himself like this child
is the greatest in the kingdom of heaven."
- *Matt. 18:4 NIV* -

Humility is not an ideal, it is the unconscious
result of the life being rightly related to God.
- *Oswald Chambers* -

Husband

hus · band /'hʌzbənd/ *noun*

1. A man joined to another person in marriage; a male spouse. 2. A woman's partner in marriage, your best friend, mate, lover.

A wife of noble character is her husband's crown, but a disgraceful wife is like decay in his bones.
- Prov. 12:4 NIV -

Love each other with genuine affection, and take delight in honoring each other.
- Rom. 12:10 NLT -

Wives, submit to your own husbands, as to the Lord.
- Eph. 5:22 ESV -

A woman who treasures, respects and honors her husband is a queen in his eyes.
- Anonymous -

Identity

i · den · ti · ty /aɪˈdentəti/ *noun*

1. The set of characteristics by which a person is definitively recognizable or known. 2. The set of behavioral or personal characteristics by which an individual is recognizable as a member of a group. 3. Name, individuality, character, existence, distinction, originality.

········· ❀ ·········

He chose us in Him before the creation
of the world to be holy and blameless in
His sight. In love He predestined us to be
adopted as His sons through Jesus Christ,
in accordance with His pleasure and will.
- *Eph. 1:4-5* NIV -

You are a holy people, who belong to the Lord your
God. Of all the people on earth, the Lord your God
has chosen you to be His own special treasure.
- *Deut. 7:6* NLT -

Therefore, if anyone is in Christ, he is a new
creation; the old has gone, the new has come!
- *2 Cor. 5:17* NIV -

The value of identity of course
is that so often with it comes purpose.
- *Richard R. Grant* -

Inspiration

in · spi · ra · tion /ˌɪnspəˈreɪʃn/ *noun*

1. Stimulation of the mind or emotions to a high level of feeling or activity. **2.** The condition of being so stimulated. **3.** Something, such as a sudden creative act or idea, that is inspired. **4.** The quality of inspiring or exalting. **5.** Divine guidance or influence exerted directly on the mind and soul of humankind.

·········  ·········

Look to the Lord and His strength;
seek His face always.
- 1 Chron. 16:11 NIV -

I say to myself, "The Lord is my inheritance;
therefore, I will hope in Him!"
- Lam. 3:24 NLT -

We have received God's Spirit (not
the world's spirit), so we can know the
wonderful things God has freely given us.
- 1 Cor. 2:12 NLT -

Dare to be remarkable!
- Anonymous -

Integrity

in · teg · ri · ty/ɪnˈtegrəti/*noun*

1. Steadfast adherence to a strict moral or ethical code. 2. The state of being unimpaired; soundness. 3. The quality or condition of being whole or undivided; completeness. 4. The quality of being honest and having strong moral principles. 5. Righteousness, truthfulness, trustworthiness, incorruptibility, uprightness, reputability.

I know, my God, that You test the
heart and are pleased with integrity.
- *1 Chron. 29:17 NIV* -

May integrity and honesty protect me,
for I put my hope in You.
- *Ps. 25:21 NLT* -

Joyful are people of integrity,
who follow the instructions of the Lord.
- *Ps. 119:1 NLT* -

Integrity is keeping my commitments
even if the circumstances when I made
those commitments have changed.
- *David Jeremiah* -

Jesus

Je · sus /ˈdʒiːzəs/ *noun*

1. Immanuel, Deliverer, Good Shepherd, Jesus of Nazareth, Redeemer, Savior, the Nazarene, Son of God. 2. Light of the World, Lamb of God, Bread of Life, Lord of lords and King of kings.

If we walk in the light, as He is in the light, we have fellowship with one another, and the blood of Jesus purifies us from all sin.
- *1 John 1:7* NIV -

Jesus replied, "I am the bread of life. Whoever comes to Me will never be hungry again. Whoever believes in Me will never be thirsty."
- *John 6:35* NLT -

Let us fix our eyes on Jesus, the author and perfecter of our faith, who for the joy set before Him endured the cross.
- *Heb. 12:2* NIV -

How sweet the name of Jesus sounds in a believer's ear; It soothes his sorrows, heals his wounds, and drives away his fear.

- *John Newton* -

Joy

joy/dʒɔɪ/*noun*

1. The expression or manifestation of happiness found in the Lord. 2. A source or an object of pleasure or satisfaction. 3. To take great pleasure; rejoice. 4. To enjoy, joyfulness, joyousness, exultation, jubilance, delight, pleasure.

The joy of the Lord is your strength.
- *Neh. 8:10* NIV -

This is the day the Lord has made;
let us rejoice and be glad in it.
- *Ps. 118:24* NIV -

You make known to me the path of life;
in Your presence there is fullness of joy;
at Your right hand are pleasures forevermore.
- *Ps. 16:11* ESV -

There is more joy in Jesus in twenty-four
hours than there is in the world in 365 days.
I have tried them both.
- *R. A. Torrey* -

Kindness

kind · ness/ˈkaɪndnəs/*noun*

1. The practice or quality of being kind 2. A kind, considerate, or helpful act. 3. The quality of being warmhearted, considerate, humane and sympathetic. 4. Generosity, loving-kindness, thoughtfulness, consideration, goodness.

....  ....

Since God chose you to be the holy people whom He loves, you must clothe yourself with tenderhearted mercy, kindness, humility, gentleness, and patience. Remember, the Lord forgave you, so you must forgive others.
- Col. 3:12-13 NLT -

An excellent wife who can find? She is far more precious than jewels. She opens her mouth with wisdom, and the teaching of kindness is on her tongue.
- Prov. 31:10, 26 ESV -

"I love you people with a love that will last forever. That is why I have continued showing you kindness."
- Jer. 31:3 NCV -

Kindness is the sunshine in which virtue grows.
- Robert Green Ingersoll -

Life

life /laɪf/ *noun*

1. A living being, especially a person. 2. The physical, mental, and spiritual experiences that constitute existence. 3. The interval of time between birth and death. 4. A particular segment of one's life. 5. An account of a person's life; a biography.

"Choose to love the Lord your God
and to obey Him and to commit
yourself to Him, for He is your life."
- *Deut. 30:20* NLT -

Whoever finds Me finds life
and receives favor from the Lord.
- *Prov. 8:35* NLT -

"My child, listen and accept what I say.
Then you will have a long life."
- *Prov. 4:10* NCV -

This life is worth living, we can say,
since it is what we make it.
- *William James* -

Listening

lis · ten · ing /'lɪsnɪŋ/ *noun*

1. The act of hearing attentively. 2. Hearing, sensing, perception, rehearing.

My child, listen to me and treasure my instructions. Then you will understand what is right, just and fair.
- *Prov. 2:1, 9* NLT -

He who listens to reproof gains intelligence.
- *Prov. 15:32* ESV -

Listen closely to everything I say. Be careful to obey. Then all will go well with you.
- *Deut. 6:3* NLT -

Too often we underestimate the power of a touch, a smile, a kind word, a listening ear, an honest compliment, or the smallest act of caring, all of which have the potential to turn a life around.

- *Leo Buscaglia* -

Love

love /lʌv/ *noun*

1. A deep, tender feeling of affection toward a person, such as that arising from kinship, recognition of attractive qualities, or a sense of underlying oneness. 2. A feeling of intense desire and attraction toward a person. 3. An intense emotional attachment. 4. The love of God or Christ for mankind, devotedness, devotion.

········· ❁ ·········

Now these three remain: faith, hope and love. But the greatest of these is love.
- *1 Cor. 13:13 NIV* -

Love is patient and kind. It is not irritable, and it keeps no record of being wronged. Love never gives up, never loses faith, is always hopeful, and endures through every circumstance.
- *1 Cor. 13:4-5, 7 NLT* -

I am sure that neither death, nor life, nor angels, nor ruling spirits, nothing now, nothing in the future, no powers, nothing above us, nothing below us, nor anything else in the whole world will ever be able to separate us from the love of God that is in Christ Jesus our Lord.
- *Rom. 8:38-39 NCV* -

You will find as you look back upon your life that the moments when you have really lived, are the moments when you have done things in a spirit of love.

- *Henry Drummond* -

Marriage

mar · riage/'mærɪdʒ/*noun*

1. The legal union of a man and woman as husband and wife, usually entailing legal obligations of each person to the other. **2.** The state or relationship between a man and a woman who are married.

·········  ·········

Most important of all, continue to show deep love for each other for love covers a multitude of sins.
- 1 Pet. 4:8 NLT -

Give honor to marriage, and remain faithful to one another in marriage.
- Heb. 13:4 NLT -

May the patience and encouragement that come from God allow you to live in harmony with each other the way Christ Jesus wants. Then you will be joined together, and you will give glory to God.
- Rom. 15:5-6 NCV -

Be the mate God designed you to be.
- Anthony T. Evans -

Mercy

mer · cy/ˈmɜːrsi/*noun*

1. Compassionate treatment, especially of those under one's power. 2. A disposition to be kind and forgiving. 3. Something for which to be thankful; a blessing. 4. Compassion, charity, pity, forgiveness, favor, grace, kindness.

Mercy to the needy is a loan to God,
and God pays back those loans in full.
- *Prov. 19:17* MSG -

May God be merciful and bless us.
May His face smile with favor on us.
- *Ps. 67:1* NLT -

He saved us, not because of righteous
things we had done, but because of His mercy.
- *Titus 3:5* NIV -

Where mercy, love, and pity dwell,
there God is dwelling too.
- *William Blake* -

Miracles

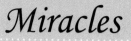

mi·ra·cles /ˈmɪrəkls/ *noun*

1. An event that appears inexplicable by the laws of nature and an act of God. 2. Any amazing or wonderful event.

"If you believe, you will receive whatever you ask for in prayer."
- *Matt. 21:22* NIV -

"Everything is possible for him who believes."
- *Mark 9:23* NIV -

I can do everything through Christ, who gives me strength.
- *Phil. 4:13* NLT -

Miracles are a retelling in small letters of the very same story which is written across the whole world in letters too large for some of us to see.
- *C. S. Lewis* -

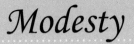

Modesty

mod · es · ty /ˈmaːdəsti/ *noun*

1. The state or quality of being modest 2. Lack of pretentiousness; simplicity.

"Whoever humbles himself like this child
is the greatest in the kingdom of heaven."
- *Matt. 18:4 NIV* -

He who is lowly in spirit will obtain honor.
- *Prov. 29:23 ESV* -

He shows those who are humble how to
do right, and He teaches them His ways.
- *Ps. 25:9 NCV* -

Great modesty often hides great merit.
- *Benjamin Franklin* -

Motherhood

moth · er · hood /ˈmʌðərhʊd/ *noun*

1. The state of being a mother. 2. The qualities of a mother, The headliner in God's great vaudeville. 3. Sacrifice, being a role mode, a secret-keeper, a comforter, a friend.

Her children arise and call her blessed;
her husband also, and he praises her.
- Prov. 31:28 NIV -

Children are a gift from the Lord;
babies are a reward.
- Ps. 127:3 NCV -

Nothing gives me greater joy than to hear that
my children are following the way of truth.
- 3 John 4 NCV -

If you have a mom, there is nowhere you are
likely to go where a prayer has not already been.
- Robert Brault -

Obedience

o · be · di · ence /əˈbiːdiəns/ *noun*

**1. The condition or quality of being obedient.
2. The act or an instance of obeying; dutiful or
submissive behavior 3. The authority vested in
a Church or similar body. 4. Compliance, yield-
ing, submission, respect.**

·········· ❀ ··········

"Even more blessed are those who hear
God's Word and guard it with their lives!"
- Luke 11:28 MSG -

Share each other's burdens,
and in this way obey the law of Christ.
- Gal. 6:2 NLT -

"When you obey My commandments,
you remain in My love, just as I obey My
Father's commandments and remain in His love.
I have told you these things so that you will be
filled with My joy. Yes, your joy will overflow!"
- John 15:10-11 NLT -

One act of obedience is better
than one hundred sermons.

- Dietrich Bonhoeffer -

Patience

pa · tience /ˈpeɪʃns/ *noun*

1. Tolerant and even-tempered perseverance
2. The capacity for calmly enduring pain, trying situations. 3. Forbearance, tolerance, composure, serenity.

Be joyful because you have hope. Be patient when trouble comes, and pray at all times.
- *Rom. 12:12* NCV -

Always be humble, gentle, and patient, accepting each other in love.
- *Eph. 4:2* NCV -

God blesses those who patiently endure testing and temptation. Afterward they will receive the crown of life that God has promised to those who love Him.
- *James 1:12* NLT -

Patience is the companion of wisdom.
- *St. Augustine* -

Peace

peace/piːs/*noun*

1. Inner contentment, serenity, calm, relaxation, composure, contentment. 2. The absence of war or other hostilities 2. Freedom from quarrels and disagreement; harmonious relations.

"I am leaving you with a gift – peace of mind and heart. And the peace I give is a gift the world cannot give. So don't be troubled or afraid."
- *John 14:27* NLT -

May the Lord watch over you and give you peace.
- *Num. 6:26* NCV -

May the Lord of peace give you
peace at all times and in every way.
- *2 Thess. 3:16* NCV -

If God be our God, He will give us peace in trouble: when there is a storm without, He will make music within. The world can create trouble in peace, but God can create peace in trouble.

- *Thomas Watson* -

Perseverance

per · se · ver · ance/ˌpɜːrsəˈvɪrəns/*noun*

1. Steady persistence in adhering to a course of action, a belief, or a purpose; steadfastness. 2. That those who have been chosen by God will continue in a state of grace to the end and will finally be saved. 3. Persistence, resolution, determination, dedication, stamina, endurance, tenacity.

Consider it pure joy whenever you face
trials of many kinds, because you know that
the testing of your faith develops perseverance.
- James 1:2-4 NIV -

Let us throw off everything that hinders and
the sin that so easily entangles, and let us run
with perseverance the race marked out for us.
- Heb. 12:1 NIV -

You need to persevere so that when
you have done the will of God, you
will receive what He has promised.
- Heb. 10:36 NIV -

Few things are impossible to
diligence and skill. Great works are
performed, not by strength, but perseverance.
- Samuel Johnson -

Planning

plan · ning/'plænɪŋ/*noun*

1. An act of formulating a program for a definite course of action. 2. Arrangement, organization, setting up, working out, preparation.

The plans of the Lord stand firm forever,
the purposes of His heart through all generations.
- Ps. 33:11 NIV -

We can make our plans,
but the Lord determines our steps.
- Prov. 16:9 NLT -

Because we are united with Christ,
we have received an inheritance from God,
for He chose us in advance, and He makes
everything work out according to His plan.
- Eph. 1:11 NLT -

In preparing for battle I have always found
that plans are useless, but planning is indispensable.
- Dwight D. Eisenhower -

Praise

praise/preɪz/*tr verb*

1. To express commendation, admiration.
2. To proclaim or describe the glorious attributes of God with homage and thanksgiving.
3. Worship, bless, adore, magnify, glorify, exalt.

....  ....

Lord, I will honor and praise Your name,
for You are my God. You do such wonderful
things! You planned them long ago, and
now You have accomplished them.
- Isa. 25:1 NLT -

Sing to the Lord a new song,
for He has done marvelous things.
- Ps. 98:1 NIV -

Lord, I will praise You among the nations;
I will sing praises to Your name.
You show unfailing love to Your anointed.
- Ps. 18:49-50 NLT -

The most valuable thing the Psalms
do for me is to express the same delight
in God which made David dance.
- C. S. Lewis -

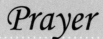

Prayer

prayer/prer/*noun*

1. A reverent petition made to God. 2. An act of communion with God such as in devotion, confession, praise, or thanksgiving. 3. A specially worded form used to address God.

When a believing person prays, great things happen.
- *James 5:16 NCV* -

"Ask and it will be given to you; seek and you will find; knock and the door will be opened to you."
- *Matt. 7:7 NIV* -

Don't quit in hard times; pray all the harder.
- *Rom. 12:12 MSG* -

When I stop praying, the
"coincidences" stop happening.
- *William Temple* -

Priorities

pri · or · i · ties/praɪˈɔːrətis/*noun*

1. Precedence, especially established by order of importance or urgency. 2. An established right to precedence. 3. A preceding or coming earlier in time. 4. Something afforded or deserving prior attention.

"Where your treasure is,
there your heart will be also."
- Matt. 6:21 NIV -

"No one can serve two masters.
Either he will hate the one and love the other,
or he will be devoted to the one and despise the
other. You cannot serve both God and Money."
- Matt. 6:24 NIV -

"Whoever would save his life will lose it,
but whoever loses his life for My sake will find it."
- Matt. 16:24-26 ESV -

You can't get second things by putting them first; you can get second things only by putting first things first.
- C. S. Lewis -

Protection

pro · tec · tion/prəˈtekʃn/*noun*

1. The act of protecting. **2.** The condition of
being protected. **3.** Safety, charge, care, defense,
protecting, security, guarding.

He has put His angels in charge of you to watch over
you wherever you go. They will catch you in their
hands so that you will not hit your foot on a rock.
- *Ps. 91:11-12 NCV* -

The Lord keeps you from all harm and watches
over your life. The Lord keeps watch over you
as you come and go, both now and forever.
- *Ps. 121:7-8 NLT* -

The name of the Lord is a strong tower;
the righteous run to it and are safe.
- *Prov. 18:10 NIV* -

Safety does not depend on our conception
of the absence of danger. Safety is found in
God's presence, in the center of His perfect will.
- *T. J. Bach* -

Provision

pro · vi · sion/prəˈvɪʒn/*noun*

1. The activity of supplying or providing something. **2.** Giving, supplying, sustenance.

"Your Father knows exactly what you
need even before you ask Him!"
- Matt. 6:8 NLT -

My God will use His wonderful riches in Christ
Jesus to give you everything you need. Glory to
our God and Father forever and ever! Amen.
- Phil. 4:19-20 NCV -

The Lord is my shepherd, I shall not be in want.
He makes me lie down in green pastures,
He leads me beside quiet waters, He restores my soul.
- Ps. 23:1-3 NIV -

God loves and cares for us, even to
the least event and smallest need of life.
- Henry Edward Manning -

Purpose

pur · pose /ˈpɜːrpəs/ *noun*

1. The reason for which anything is done, created, or exists. 2. A fixed design, outcome, or idea that is the object of an action or other effort. 3. Fixed intention in doing something; determination. 4. Reason, point, idea, goal, aim, principle, function, intention, objective, motivation, commitment.

.... ❋ ....

The Lord will fulfill His purpose for me;
Your love, O Lord, endures forever.
- *Ps. 138:8 NIV* -

Trust the Lord with all your heart, and don't depend on your own understanding. Remember the Lord in all you do, and He will give you success.
- *Prov. 3:5-6 NCV* -

The Lord has told you what is good, and this is what He requires of you: to do what is right, to love mercy, and to walk humbly with your God.
- *Mic. 6:8 NLT* -

The purpose of life ... is a life of purpose.

- *Anonymous* -

Relationships

re · la · tion · ships /rɪˈleɪʃnʃɪps/ *noun*

1. The condition or fact of being related; connection or association. 2. Connection by blood or marriage; kinship. 3. A particular type of connection existing between people related to or having dealings with each other. 4. Association, bond, communications, connection.

....  ....

"I tell you that if two of you on earth agree about anything you ask for, it will be done for you by My Father in heaven. For where two or three come together in My name, there am I with them."
- *Matt. 18:19-20 NIV* -

Two are better than one, because they have a good return for their work: If one falls down, his friend can help him up. Though one may be overpowered, two can defend themselves. A cord of three strands is not quickly broken.
- *Eccles. 4:9-10, 12 NIV* -

Share each other's troubles and problems, and in this way obey the law of Christ.
- *Gal. 6:2 NLT* -

You can never establish a personal relationship without opening up your own heart.
- *Paul Tournier* -

Renewal

re · new · al /rɪˈnuːəl/ *noun*

1. The act of renewing or the state of having been renewed. 2. Something renewed. 3. Restoration, transformation.

Let the Spirit renew your thoughts and attitudes.
Put on your new nature, created to be like God –
truly righteous and holy.
- Eph. 4:23-24 NLT -

If anyone belongs to Christ, there is a new creation.
The old things have gone; everything is made new!
- 2 Cor. 5:17 NCV -

The God of all grace, who called you to His
eternal glory in Christ, will Himself restore
you and make you strong, firm and steadfast.
- 1 Pet. 5:10 NIV -

Above all, believe confidently that Jesus delights
in maintaining that new nature within you, and
imparting to it His strength and wisdom for its work.
- Andrew Murray -

Respect

re · spect/rɪˈspekt/*noun*

1. An attitude of admiration, or esteem; regard.
2. The state of being honored or esteemed.
3. Polite or kind regard; consideration.
4. Honor, recognition, appreciation, reverence,
estimation.

Do nothing out of selfish ambition
or vain conceit, but in humility
consider others better than yourselves.
- Phil. 2:3 NIV -

You, dear friends, must continue to build
your lives on the foundation of your holy faith.
- Jude 1:20 NLT -

Honor your father and your mother,
so that you may live long in the land
the Lord your God is giving you.
- Exod. 20:12 NIV -

Without respect, love cannot go far or rise high:
it is an angel with but one wing.
- Alexander Dumas -

Rest

rest/rest/*verb*

1. To place or position oneself for rest or relaxation. 2. Sleep, take it easy, lie down, idle, nap, be calm, doze, sit down. 3. Be at ease, put your feet up, take a nap, refresh yourself.

....  ....

"Come to Me, all who labor and are heavy laden, and I will give you rest. You will find rest for your souls."
- *Matt. 11:28-29 ESV* -

I can lie down and go to sleep, and I will wake up again, because the Lord gives me strength.
- *Ps. 3:5 NCV* -

Whoever dwells in the shelter of the Most High will rest in the shadow of the Almighty.
- *Ps. 91:1 NIV* -

You have created us for Yourself, and our heart cannot be stilled until it finds rest in You.
- *St. Augustine* -

Rewards

re · wards /rɪˈwɔːrds / *noun*

1. Something given or received in recompense for worthy behavior. 2. A satisfying return or result.

"Be strong and do not give up,
for your work will be rewarded."
- *2 Chron. 15:7 NIV* -

"If anyone gives even a cup of cold water to one
of these little ones because he is My disciple, I tell
you the truth, he will certainly not lose his reward."
- *Matt. 10:42 NIV* -

Being kind to the poor is like lending to the Lord;
He will reward you for what you have done.
- *Prov. 19:17 NCV* -

Before the reward there must be labor. You plant before you harvest. You sow in tears before you reap joy.
- *Ralph Ransom* -

Righteousness

right · eous · ness /ˈraɪtʃəsnəs/ *noun*

1. Adhering to moral principles; impeccability, rectitude, uprightness, piety, piousness. 2. Morality, justice, justness, honorableness, honor, honesty.

Light is shed upon the righteous
and joy on the upright in heart.
- *Ps. 97:11* NIV -

For surely, O Lord, You bless the righteous;
You surround them with Your favor as with a shield.
- *Ps. 5:12* NIV -

"Seek the Kingdom of God above all else,
and live righteously, and He will give
you everything you need."
- *Matt. 6:33* NLT -

The righteousness of Jesus Christ is one
of those great mysteries, which the angels desire
to look into, and seems to be one of the first
lessons that God taught men after the fall.

- *George Whitefield* -

Sacrifice

sac · ri · fice /'sækrɪfaɪs/ *noun*

1. A surrender of something of value as a means of gaining something more desirable or of preventing some evil. 2. Surrender, giving up, offering our lives to God's service.

....  ....

Live a life of love just as Christ
loved us and gave Himself for us as a
sweet-smelling offering and sacrifice to God.
- Eph. 5:2 NCV -

Don't forget to do good and to share
what you have with those in need, for
such sacrifices are very pleasing to God.
- Heb. 13:16 NLT -

This is love: not that we loved God,
but that He loved us and sent His
Son as an atoning sacrifice for our sins.
- 1 John 4:10 NIV -

I believe that every sacrifice we make will
so enrich us in the future that our regret will
be that we did not enrich the sacrifice the more.
- George F. Burba -

Savior

Sav · ior /ˈseɪvjər/ *noun*

....  ....

1. Jesus, Son of God, Deliverer, Good Shepherd, Jesus Christ, Jesus of Nazareth, Redeemer, the Nazarene.

"For God so loved the world that He gave His one and only Son, that whoever believes in Him shall not perish but have eternal life."
- *John 3:16* NIV -

"When you go through deep waters, I will be with you. When you go through rivers of difficulty, you will not drown. For I am the Lord … your Savior."
- *Isa. 43:2-3* NLT -

To the only God our Savior be glory, majesty, power and authority, through Jesus Christ our Lord, before all ages, now and forevermore!
- *Jude 25* NIV -

Jesus is moved to happiness every time He sees that you appreciate what He has done for you. Grip His pierced hand and say to Him, "I thank Thee, Savior, because Thou hast died for me."
- *O. Hallesby* -

Security

se·cu·ri·ty /səˈkjʊrəti/ *noun*

1. Freedom from risk or danger; safety. 2. Freedom from doubt, anxiety, or fear; confidence.

The name of the Lord is a strong tower;
the righteous run to it and are safe.
- Prov. 18:10 NIV -

God did not give us a spirit of timidity,
but a spirit of power, of love and of self-discipline.
- 2 Tim. 1:7 NIV -

"Fear not, for I am with you; be not dismayed,
for I am your God; I will strengthen you, I will
uphold you with My righteous right hand."
- Isa. 41:10 ESV -

Nothing can bring a real sense of security
into the home except true love.
- Billy Graham -

Self-control

self · con · trol/self–kənˈtroʊl/*noun*

1. Control of one's emotions, desires, or actions by one's own will. 2. Self-discipline, control, willpower, restraint, calmness, self-restraint, self-mastery, strength of mind.

Above all else, guard your heart,
for it affects everything you do.
- *Prov. 4:23* NLT -

Knowing God leads to self-control.
Self-control leads to patient endurance,
and patient endurance leads to godliness.
- *2 Pet. 1:6* NLT -

God gave us a spirit not of fear but
of power and love and self-control.
- *2 Tim. 1:7* ESV -

If you are to be self-controlled in your speech
you must be self-controlled in your thinking.

- *Francois Fénelon* -

Self-worth

self · worth /self–wɜːrθ/ *noun*

1. The quality of being worthy of esteem or respect, dignity, self-regard. 2. Self-esteem, self-respect.

What are people that You should think about them, mere mortals that You should care for them? Yet You made them only a little lower than God and crowned them with glory and honor.

- Ps. 8:3-5 NLT -

You made all the delicate, inner parts of my body and knit me together in my mother's womb.

- Ps. 139:13 NLT -

"I knew you before I formed you in your mother's womb. Before you were born I set you apart."

- Jer. 1:5 NLT -

Aerodynamically the bumblebee shouldn't be able to fly, but the bumblebee doesn't know that so it goes on flying anyway.

- Mary Kay Ash -

Sex

sex/seks/noun

1. Sexual intercourse between a man and a woman as ordained by God. 2. Procreation.

....  ....

"A man shall leave his father and mother and hold fast to his wife, and the two shall become one flesh."
- *Eph. 5:31* ESV -

Give honor to marriage, and remain faithful to one another in marriage. God will surely judge people who are immoral and those who commit adultery.
- *Heb. 13:4* NLT -

Each one of you must love his wife as he loves himself, and a wife must respect her husband.
- *Eph. 5:33* NCV -

Passion is the quickest to develop,
and the quickest to fade. Intimacy develops
more slowly, and commitment more gradually still.

- *Robert Sternberg* -

Strength

strength/streŋθ/*noun*

1. The state, property, or quality of being strong. 2. The power to resist strain or stress; durability. 3. The ability to maintain a moral or intellectual position firmly. 4. Will, spirit, courage, character, determination, stamina, toughness, tenacity, willpower.

....  ....

The people who trust the Lord will become strong again. They will rise up as an eagle in the sky; they will run and not need rest; they will walk and not become tired.
- Isa. 40:31 NCV -

God arms me with strength, and He makes my way perfect.
- Ps. 18:32 NLT -

The Lord gives me strength and makes me sing; He has saved me. He is my God, and I will praise Him. He is the God of my ancestors, and I will honor Him.
- Exod. 15:2 NCV -

We can be tired, weary and emotionally distraught, but after spending time alone with God, we find that He injects into our bodies energy, power and strength.
- Charles Stanley -

Stress

stress /stres/ *noun*

1. Special emphasis or significance attached to something. 2. Mental, emotional, or physical strain or tension. 3. Tenseness, mental strain, nervous strain.

Give your burdens to the Lord, and He will take care of you. He will not permit the godly to slip and fall.
- *Ps. 55:22 NLT* -

Those who trust in the Lord are like Mount Zion, which cannot be shaken but endures forever.
- *Ps. 125:1 NIV* -

"So do not worry, saying, 'What shall we eat?' or 'What shall we drink?' or 'What shall we wear?' For the pagans run after all these things, and your heavenly Father knows that you need them."
- *Matt. 6:31-32 NIV* -

One of the best ways to counteract stress is to pray for others.

- *Anonymous* -

Success

suc · cess /sək'ses/ *noun*

1. The achievement of something desired, planned, or attempted. 2. An event that accomplishes its intended purpose, triumph, victory.

·········  ·········

May God give you what you want
and make all your plans succeed.
- *Ps. 20:4 NCV* -

It is not that we think we can do
anything of lasting value by ourselves.
Our only power and success come from God.
- *2 Cor. 3:5 NLT* -

Respecting the Lord and not being
proud will bring you wealth, honor, and life.
- *Prov. 22:4 NCV* -

God gave us two ends, one to sit on and the other
to think with. Success depends upon which end
we use the most. Heads, we win. Tails, we lose.

- *Anonymous* -

Support

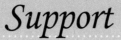

sup · port /səˈpɔːrt/ *tr. verb*

1. To be capable of bearing; withstand. 2. To keep from weakening or failing; strengthen. 3. Help, protection, comfort, friendship, assistance, blessing, loyalty, moral support.

"I am with you always, to the very end of the age."
- *Matt. 28:20* NIV -

"My Presence will go with you,
and I will give you rest."
- *Exod. 33:14* NIV -

"I am leaving you with a gift – peace of mind
and heart. And the peace I give isn't like the peace
the world gives. So don't be troubled or afraid."
- *John 14:27* NLT -

I know God will not give me anything I can't handle.
I just wish that He didn't trust me so much.

- *Mother Teresa* -

Surrender

sur · ren · der /sə'rendər/ *tr. verb*

1. To relinquish possession or control of to another because of demand or compulsion. 2. To give up in favor of another. 3. Submission, give yourself over to God completely.

Give your burdens to the Lord,
and He will take care of you. He will
not permit the godly to slip and fall.
- *Ps. 55:22* NLT -

Give all your worries and cares
to God, for He cares about you.
- *1 Pet. 5:7* NLT -

Letting the Spirit control your
mind leads to life and peace.
- *Rom. 8:6* NLT -

Every evening, I turn my worries over to God.
He's going to be up all night anyway.
- *Mary C. Crowley* -

Teamwork

team · work /ˈtiːmwɜːrk/ *noun*

1. Cooperative effort by the members of a group or team to achieve a common goal. 2. Cooperation, collaboration, unity, concert, harmony, fellowship.

Share each other's troubles and problems, and in this way obey the law of Christ.
- *Gal. 6:2* NLT -

Let us not give up meeting together, as some are in the habit of doing, but let us encourage one another – and all the more as you see the Day approaching.
- *Heb. 10:25* NIV -

Two are better than one, because they have a good reward for their toil. For if they fall, one will lift up his fellow.
- *Eccles. 4:9-10* ESV -

Individual commitment to a group effort – that is what makes a team work, a company work, a society work, a civilization work.
- *Vince Lombardi* -

Thanksgiving

thanks · giv · ing /ˌθæŋksˈɡɪvɪŋ/ *noun*

1. An act of giving thanks; an expression of gratitude, especially to God. 2. An expression of thanks to God.

....  ....

Give thanks to the Lord, for He is good!
His faithful love endures forever.
- 1 Chron. 16:34 NLT -

How we thank God, who gives us victory over sin and death through Jesus Christ our Lord!
- 1 Cor. 15:57 NLT -

Thanks be to God, who always leads us in triumphal procession in Christ and through us spreads everywhere the fragrance of the knowledge of Him.
- 2 Cor. 2:14 NIV -

Thanksgiving is a good thing: thanksliving is better.
- Anonymous -

Time

time/taɪm/*noun*

1. A continuous, measurable quantity in which events occur in a sequence proceeding from the past through the present to the future.

I love Your clear-cut revelation. You're my place of quiet retreat; I wait for Your Word to renew me.
- *Ps. 119:115 MSG* -

"Live in Me. Make your home in Me. If you make yourselves at home with Me and My words are at home in you, you can be sure that whatever you ask will be listened to and acted upon."
- *John 15:4,7 MSG* -

Pray to God – my life a prayer – and wait for what He'll say and do. My life's on the line before God, my Lord, waiting and watching till morning.
- *Ps. 130:5-6 MSG* -

The future is something which everyone reaches at the rate of sixty minutes an hour, whatever he does, whoever he is.
- *C. S. Lewis* -

Trust

trust/trʌst/*noun*

1. Firm reliance on the integrity, ability, or character of a person or thing. 2. Believe in, have faith in, depend on, count on. 3. Confidence, credit, belief, faith, expectation.

"Do not let your hearts be troubled.
Trust in God; trust also in Me."
- John 14:1 NIV -

Let the morning bring me word of
Your unfailing love, for I have put my trust in You.
- Ps. 143:8 NIV -

The Lord is good, a stronghold in the day of
trouble; He knows those who take refuge in Him.
- Nah. 1:7 ESV -

Trust God for great things; with your five loaves and
two fishes, He will show you a way to feed thousands.
- Horace Bushnell -

Understanding

un · der · stand · ing /ˌʌndərˈstændɪŋ/ *noun*

1. The quality or condition of one who understands. 2. The faculty by which one understands; intelligence. 3. Individual or specified judgment or outlook; opinion. 4. Discernment, apprehension, comprehension. 5. Knowledge, grasp, sense, know-how.

········· ❀ ·········

Give me an understanding mind so that I can …
know the difference between right and wrong.
- *1 Kings 3:9 NLT* -

If you call out for insight and raise your
voice for understanding, if you seek it like
silver and search for it as for hidden treasures,
then you will find the knowledge of God.
- *Prov. 2:3-5 ESV* -

The unfolding of Your words gives light;
it gives understanding to the simple.
- *Ps. 119:130 NIV* -

Having someone who understands is a
great blessing for ourselves. Being someone
who understands is a great blessing to others.
- *Janette Oke* -

Victory

vic · to · ry /'vɪktəri/ *noun*

1. The state of having triumphed. 2. Defeat of an enemy or opponent. 3. Success in a struggle against difficulties or an obstacle.

> We are more than conquerors
> through Him who loved us.
> *- Rom. 8:37 NIV -*

> With God we will gain the victory,
> and He will trample down our enemies.
> *- Ps. 60:12 NIV -*

> Yours, O Lord, is the greatness,
> the power, the glory, the victory, and the majesty.
> Everything in the heavens and on earth
> is Yours, O Lord, and this is Your kingdom.
> We adore You as the one who is over all things.
> *- 1 Chron. 29:11 NLT -*

When we pray for the Spirit's help ... we will simply fall down at the Lord's feet in our weakness. There we will find the victory and power that comes from His love.

- Andrew Murray -

Wisdom

wis · dom/ˈwɪzdəm/*noun*

1. The ability to discern or judge what is true, right, or lasting; insight. 2. Common sense; good judgment. 3. The sum of learning through the ages; knowledge.

·········  ·········

The Lord gives wisdom, and from His
mouth come knowledge and understanding.
- Prov. 2:6 NIV -

If you need wisdom – if you want to know
what God wants you to do – ask Him
and He will gladly tell you.
- James 1:5 NLT -

Teach us to number our days aright,
that we may gain a heart of wisdom.
- Ps. 90:12 NIV -

Wisdom is knowledge applied.
Head knowledge is useless on the battlefield.
Knowledge stamped on the heart makes one wise.
- Beth Moore -

Work

work/wɜːrk/*noun*

1. Physical or mental effort or activity directed toward the production or accomplishment of something. 2. A job; employment, a trade, profession, or other means of livelihood.

The Lord blesses you with bountiful harvests
and gives you success in all your work.
- *Deut. 16:15* NLT -

I run with purpose in every step. I am not
just shadowboxing. I discipline my body
like an athlete, training it to do what it should.
- *1 Cor. 9:26-27* NLT -

All glory to God, who is able, through His
mighty power at work within us, to accomplish
infinitely more than what we might ask or think.
- *Eph. 3:20* NLT -

Choose a job you love, and you
will never have to work a day in your life.
- *Confucius* -

Worship

wor · ship/ˈwɜːrʃɪp/*verb*

1. To show profound devotion and respect to God. 2. To be devoted to and full of admiration for. 3. To attend services for worship, glorify, reverence, venerate.

Give honor to the Lord for the glory of His name. Worship the Lord in the splendor of His holiness.
- *Ps. 29:2* NLT -

So here's what I want you to do,
God helping you: Take your everyday,
ordinary life – your sleeping, eating, going-
to-work, and walking-around life – and place it
before God as an offering. Embracing what God
does for you is the best thing you can do for Him.
- *Rom. 12:1* MSG -

The Lord is great; He should be praised.
He should be respected.
- *1 Chron. 16:25* NCV -

I never knew how to worship until I knew how to love.

- *Henry Ward Beecher* -

The Word of God on Words

.... ❋ ....

A word aptly spoken is like
apples of gold in settings of silver.

- Prov. 25:11 NIV -

Let my words and my thoughts
be pleasing to you, Lord.

- Ps. 19:14 CEV -

The words of the wise bring them praise.

- Eccles. 10:12 NCV -

Saying the right word at the
right time is so pleasing.

- Prov. 15:23 NCV -

The Word of God on Words

.... ❁ ....

Words kill, words give life; they're
either poison or fruit – you choose.
- Prov. 18:21 MSG -

Wise words bring many benefits.
- Prov. 12:14 NLT -

Gentle words are a tree of life.
- Prov. 15:4 NLT -

Kind words are like honey –
sweet to the soul and healthy to the body.
- Prov. 16:24 NLT -

Words That Have Touched My Heart . . .

.... ❀ ....

_____

_____

_____

_____

_____

_____

_____

_____

_____

_____

_____

_____